Stinky Winky Silly Willy Off-key Donkey
A Fun Rhyming Animal Bedtime Book For Kids
Really Silly Wonky Songy Children's Books Series #1
by Donald Jacobsen

an imprint of Three Suns Press
Memphis, Tennessee

All content copyright ©2018, 2019 Donald Jacobsen. All rights reserved. Without limiting the rights under the copyright reserved above, no part of this publication may be reproduced, stored in, or introduced into a retrieval system, or transmitted in any form or by any means (electronic, mechanical, photocopying, recording, or otherwise) without prior explicit written permission from the author for each use case.

For questions about acceptable use or bulk orders for schools, libraries, and institutions, please e-mail the author at donald@donaldjacobsen.com.

This is a work of fiction. All names, characters, businesses, places, events and incidents are fictitious. Any resemblance to real persons, entities, or events is purely coincidental.

ISBN 978-1-7328273-0-1 (paperback)
ISBN 978-1-7328273-3-2 (hardcover)

BISAC Subjects:
JUV002090 JUVENILE FICTION / Animals / Farm Animals
JUV009110 JUVENILE FICTION / Concepts / Sounds

This book belongs to:
_____
- - - - - - - - - - - - - - - - - -
_____

There once was an animal that lived on a farm.

This animal looked very much like a horse, but with long, funny ears and a large, round snout.

But, this was no horse at all. This was a...

Now, this wasn't just any donkey. This donkey LOVED to sing! But, his voice was out of tune.

When he brayed (that's the noise donkeys make when they sing, you know) instead of singing "hee-haw", he sang "hee-hee, haw-haw"!

He was an...

Around his neck, the donkey wore a red collar with a golden nametag that read... "WILLY".

Willy loved to tell jokes.

He was a...

Now, telling jokes and singing weren't this donkey's only hobbies.

He also loved to dance!

He was a...

After singing, telling jokes, and dancing for some time, Willy wandered upon a hot air balloon.

Willy always wanted to ride in a hot air balloon.

He looked hard at that balloon for a long time and finally got the courage to get in!

He was a...

DARING STARING
DANCING PRANCING
SILLY WILLY
OFF-KEY DONKEY!

Willy flew quite high in that hot air balloon.

He flew so high that he began to get very scared and wanted to go back down!

He was a...

FLYING CRYING
DARING STARING
DANCING PRANCING
SILLY WILLY
OFF-KEY DONKEY!

Once he landed, Willy was very, very upset.

But, he was also very thankful to be back on the ground.

He was a...

CRANKY THANKY
FLYING CRYING
DARING STARING
DANCING PRANCING
SILLY WILLY
OFF-KEY DONKEY!

After getting quite scared and upset, Willy felt a rumbly in his tummy, and he POOPED right on the ground!

EW!

He was a...

STINKY WINKY
CRANKY THANKY
FLYING CRYING
DARING STARING
DANCING PRANCING
SILLY WILLY
OFF-KEY DONKEY!

Well, after leaving a stinky poop on the ground, Willy felt much better.

He felt so good, in fact, that he laid down to take a nap.

He was a...

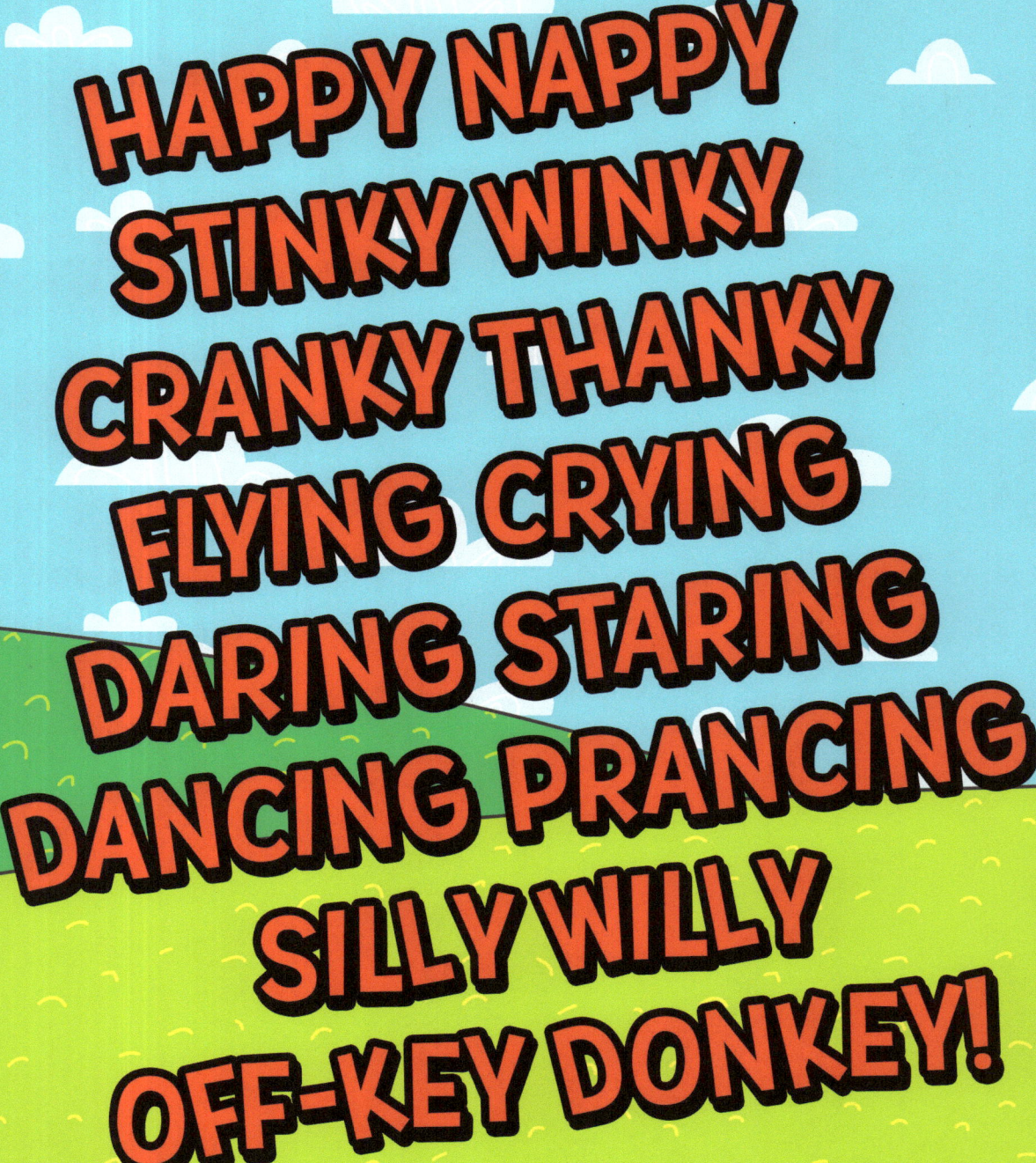

HAPPY NAPPY
STINKY WINKY
CRANKY THANKY
FLYING CRYING
DARING STARING
DANCING PRANCING
SILLY WILLY
OFF-KEY DONKEY!

Finally, Willy decided that he was done having fun for the day.

He packed up all of his things into a wagon. Willy strapped the wagon to his back, and pulled that wagon behind him all the way home.

He was a...

GOING TOWING
HAPPY NAPPY
STINKY WINKY
CRANKY THANKY
FLYING CRYING
DARING STARING
DANCING PRANCING
SILLY WILLY
OFF-KEY DONKEY!

Parents, teachers, and child educators!

We could all use more free and fun resources to help teach our kids new things. Get a totally FREE sample of some of my other books, printable coloring pages, and more! Just hop over to this link to sign up:

www.donaldjacobsen.com/freebies

If you loved this book, please leave a review with the retailer where you purchased this book. Reviews are the best thank-you that you can give an author!

About the Author

Donald Jacobsen is a dad, husband, registered nurse, and sometimes-writer living and working in Memphis, Tennessee. When not busy working on his next book, he enjoys spending time with his wife, two daughters, and their mopey rescue dog, Yoda.

Learn more at www.donaldjacobsen.com.

CPSIA information can be obtained
at www.ICGtesting.com
Printed in the USA
BVHW021916270921
617629BV00004B/206